Big Adventure

Written by Gill Budgell

zip

tug

hop off

up the net

in the mud

Talk about the book

Ask your child these questions:

1 Where is the zip wire?

2 What are the children tugging?

3 What things can you hop off?

4 What can you do to help you balance?

5 Which activity in the book would you most like to do?

6 Have you ever been to an outdoor adventure playground? What did you enjoy doing there?